HOW IT WORKS
THE WORLD OF
PLANT LIFE

Text by Gerald Legg

Illustrated by Steve Weston

HORUS EDITIONS

Published by Horus Editions Limited
1st Floor, 27 Longford Street,
London NW1 3DZ

Copyright © 2000 Horus Editions Limited

Series editor Elizabeth Miles
Text editor Helen Maxey
Designed by Paul Richards and Jenny Fry
Additional illustrations by Jim Channell

ISBN 1-899762-40-X (Cased)
ISBN 1-899762-45-0 (Paperback)

Printed in Singapore

HOW IT WORKS
CONTENTS

Plant Cells

PLANTS ARE made up of many different kinds of tiny cells. Each cell has a different job to do but all plant cells have certain parts in common. Cells are held in shape by a tough cell wall made of cellulose, which is very strong. Each cell is controlled by a nucleus, which holds all the instructions needed for the plant to live and grow. A large vacuole (storage area) holds a watery fluid under pressure, keeping the cell rigid and storing chemicals. Proteins, which are vital for carrying out many tasks, are made by ribosomes found on the endoplasmic reticulum (a network of folded membranes). Mitochondria are the cell's power stations. They convert energy stored in foods into energy which the cell can use. Chloroplasts, made of layers of membranes, contain a green pigment (colouring) called chlorophyll. Chlorophyll catches sunlight and turns it into food and energy which the plant can use.

THE GOLGI BODY PACKS UP PROTEINS MADE BY RIBOSOMES, READY TO BE STORED OR TRANSPORTED

MICROBODIES HOLD ENZYMES WHICH BREAK DOWN SUBSTANCES IN THE CELL

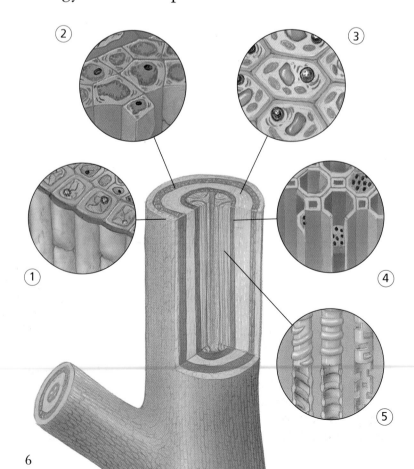

Different cell types
Epidermis cells (1) form the skin. Their outside walls are covered in a waterproof cuticle. Collenchyma cells (2) have cell walls heavily thickened with cellulose to support the plant. Parenchyma cells (3) contain chloroplasts for photosynthesis. Phloem cells (4) are thin and transport food through the plant. Xylem cells (5) are woody and joined together, forming long tubes which carry water throughout the plant.

THE VACUOLE, A LARGE BAG-LIKE AREA, HOLDS A WATERY FLUID OF DISSOLVED SALTS, SUGARS, AND PROTEINS

THE NUCLEUS, SURROUNDED BY A THIN MEMBRANE, IS THE CELL'S CONTROL CENTRE

NUCLEUS PORE

THE NUCLEOLUS, A SMALL STRUCTURE INSIDE THE NUCLEUS, PRODUCES CHEMICALS TO MAKE PROTEINS

THE ENDOPLASMIC RETICULUM MOVES SUBSTANCES AROUND INSIDE THE CELL

RIBOSOMES (ON THE ENDOPLASMIC RETICULUM) MAKE PROTEINS

TINY STRANDS THAT PASS THROUGH OPENINGS IN EACH CELL WALL LINK CELLS TOGETHER

MITOCHONDRIA PROVIDE ENERGY TO DRIVE THE CELL

THE CELL WALL HOLDS THE CELL TOGETHER

PIT FIELDS LINK CELLS

CHLOROPLASTS CONTAIN THE GREEN PIGMENT, CALLED CHLOROPHYLL, WHICH TRAPS ENERGY FROM SUNLIGHT

THE PLASMA MEMBRANE SURROUNDS THE CELL BENEATH THE CELL WALL

MICROTUBULES ARE HOLLOW TUBES THAT HELP SUPPORT THE CELL SO THAT IT KEEPS ITS SHAPE

Diatoms
The smallest plants live in water and consist of a single cell only visible through a microscope. For protection diatoms have a hard skeleton of silica, the same substance that sand is made from. They form a variety of shapes and patterns *(right)*. Diatoms living in the sea produce a large amount of the oxygen we breath.

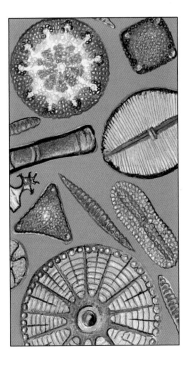

Parts of a Plant

ALTHOUGH there are many different kinds of flowering plants they are all built in a similar way. Each plant is made of millions of cells which are organized to do different jobs. Some produce food, others store it, some provide strength, and others protect the plant from pests. Groups of cells form tissues, such as wood. Different tissues work together too, forming organs. These include stems, flowers, and roots. An important set of tissues forms the vascular system, which transports food and water throughout the plant, allowing it to grow. Most plants have stems, which hold a plant up. Flowers enable plants to reproduce, and leaves make food in the form of sugars. Nearly all plants have roots that anchor them into the ground.

THE MALE AND FEMALE PARTS OF A FLOWER PRODUCE SEEDS

PETALS ARE OFTEN COLOURFUL AND ATTRACTIVE

LEAVES, FULL OF GREEN CHLOROPHYLL, MAKE FOOD USING PHOTOSYNTHESIS

VEINS CARRY FOOD FROM THE LEAVES

SIDE ROOTS GROW OUT FROM THE MAIN ROOT

MOTOR CELLS GET BIGGER AS THEY EXPAND

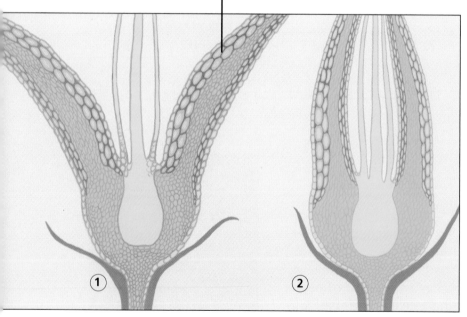

① ②

Opening flowers
Plants are not completely still – they can move parts of their bodies. Many have flowers that open during the day and close at night. Special motor cells on opposite sides of the petals can change their size. During the day those on the upper side of the petals expand while those on the lower side (1) shrink. In the evening the opposite occurs (2). These movements make flowers open and close.

A YOUNG BUD WITH SEPALS THAT GROW TIGHTLY ROUND THE PETALS

GREEN SEPALS PROTECT THE DELICATE EXPANDING PETALS

PETALS, ALMOST READY TO UNFOLD

Buds

Buds grow at the tip of branches and where leaves join the stem. Most buds form new stems and leaves, but some develop into flowers. A flower bud grows as the petals and other parts expand. Once the flower is fertilized its petals, stamens, and stigma are not needed anymore. They shrivel, die, and fall to the ground.

AS SEEDS DEVELOP, PETALS WITHER AND DIE, READY TO DROP OFF

LEAVES TAKE IN CARBON DIOXIDE TO MAKE SUGARS

A STRONG STEM CARRIES LEAVES AND FLOWERS

VASCULAR TISSUES CARRY FOOD AND WATER THROUGH-OUT THE PLANT

ROOTS GROW DOWN AND HOLD THE PLANT FIRMLY IN PLACE

ROOTS ABSORB WATER AND MINERALS

ROOTS GROW FINER AND FINER

Food flow

Inside the green parts of a plant sunlight is used to make sugars from water and carbon dioxide (a gas). This and other foods are carried in the vascular tissue throughout the plant.

Water and mineral nutrients are absorbed by the roots and carried up the plant. The water keeps the plant rigid and continually flows from the roots and out through tiny holes in the leaves.

9

Plant Leaves

THE LEAVES of plants vary in size from the tiny 2 millimetre leaves of duckweeds to the 4 metre leaves of banana plants. The main part of a leaf is the thin blade or lamina. Some leaves are a single blade while others are divided into small parts. A stalk joins the leaf blade to a stem on the plant. Veins are visible on the surface of the blade. These are tubes which carry water to and food from the leaf. Underneath the leaf tiny holes called stomata let carbon dioxide in, and oxygen and water out. The leaves act as the plant's factory. Their green colouring, called chlorophyll, traps sunlight and turns water and carbon dioxide into food. This process is called photosynthesis.

DROUGHT, DISEASE, AND WEATHER CHANGES MAKE LEAVES CHANGE COLOUR

SUNLIGHT FALLS ON THE SURFACE OF THE LEAF

MOST OF THE SUNLIGHT PASSES THROUGH THE UPPER EPIDERMIS (SKIN), SOME IS USED AND SOME IS REFLECTED

THE WATERPROOF UPPER CUTICLE

GREEN UPPER EPIDERMIS

CHLOROPLASTS MAKE THE PLANT'S FOOD

GREEN, SPONGY TISSUE LETS GASES THROUGH THE LEAF

THE LOWER EPIDERMIS IS PERFORATED BY STOMATA

WATER AND OXYGEN PASS OUT AND CARBON DIOXIDE PASSES IN

BROAD ASH LEAVES CATCH PLENTY OF SUNLIGHT

NARROW CONIFER LEAVES PROTECT THE PLANT FROM COLD AND DROUGHTS

TOUGH, SPINY HOLLY LEAVES PROTECT THE PLANT FROM BEING EATEN BY ANIMALS

Leaf types

There are many different kinds of leaves including narrow, wide, pointed, and feather-like. Each species of plant has its own type of leaf. Some leaf shapes protect the plant from cold or hot, dry climates. Others protect the plant from being eaten. Broad, drooping or pointed leaves are found in rain forests and thin, whip-like leaves in windy areas. Some leaves are even shaped as traps or enable the plant to climb.

FUNGUS DAMAGE

LEAF DAMAGE CAUSED BY
FLEA OR LEAF BEETLES

THE WASTE PRODUCT, OXYGEN,
IS GIVEN OFF THROUGH THE
UNDERSIDE OF THE LEAF

DAMAGE CAUSED BY A
TUNNELLING MOTH
CATERPILLAR

GUARD CELL OF STOMA

THE STOMATA OPENS WHEN
THE GUARD CELLS CONTRACT

THE STOMATA CLOSES WHEN
THE GUARD CELLS EXPAND

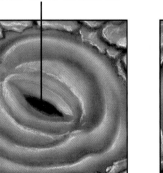

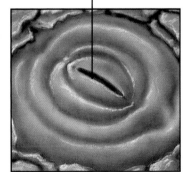

A BUNDLE SHEATH,
SURROUNDING BOTH THE
XYLEM AND PHLOEM,
FORMS A VEIN

SUGAR AND OTHER FOODS
ARE TRANSPORTED OUT OF
THE LEAF IN PHLOEM VESSELS

WATER AND MINERALS ARE
TRANSPORTED INTO THE LEAF
THROUGH XYLEM TUBES

Stomata pores
Leaves use water for photosynthesis and to help them stay rigid. To keep the water in they are waterproof. But leaves also need to take in carbon dioxide and release oxygen. Special pores under the leaves, called stomata, control the movement of these gases. When open the guard cells of the stomata let gases enter or leave. When closed they prevent too much water being lost.

Roots

ROOTS HAVE two main jobs to do. Firstly they anchor the plant firmly into the ground to stop it from falling over. Secondly they absorb water and mineral nutrients needed by the plant to grow. Some roots also act as a food store. They become fat and swollen with carbohydrates (made from the sugars that the leaves produce during photosynthesis). Special roots have other jobs to do. For example, some plants have roots for climbing, breathing, or propping up the plant.

The single root of a new plant may keep growing to become a thick, main root, or it might be replaced by a mass of thin fibrous roots. Roots usually grow down, away from the light, and towards water in the earth. So most roots grow underground. Some plants have roots that grow in the air, or ones that grow from above ground level before entering the soil.

Root tips

Roots grow at their tip. Special cells increase in number, causing the root to get longer. A tough cap of cells protects the growing tip as it forces its way through the soil. Tiny hairs grow from cells in the surface of the fine roots and take up water and nutrients from the soil. The water and nutrients pass from cell to cell and then into the xylem tubes that carry them up to the rest of the plant.

WATER AND NUTRIENTS ARE DRAWN UP THROUGH THE TREE'S ROOTS

WATER AND NUTRIENTS TRAVEL THROUGH THE XYLEM TUBES

SUGARS COME DOWN FROM THE TREE'S LEAVES TO FEED THE ROOTS

THE LEAVES AND SHOOTS OF A CARROT GROW FROM THE ROOT TOP

THE SWOLLEN MAIN ROOT OF A CARROT

A SECONDARY ROOT

A CARROT-ROOT FLY

Roots to eat

Carrots have a swollen root full of stored food that we like to eat. Insects, slugs, and wood-lice also like this food. The carrot-root fly uses carrots for food for its growing larvae (young).

WATER IS DRAWN IN FROM THE SURROUNDING SOIL PARTICLES

A HARD COVERING PROTECTS THE GROWING TIP OF THE ROOT

ROOT HAIRS ABSORB WATER

Tap root

Many plants have a single large main root. This carrot tap root grows straight down. Smaller secondary roots grow from its sides. These are very fine and absorb water and nutrients. Other plants have many fine-branched roots called fibrous roots.

SURFACE-FEEDING FIBROUS
ROOTS ABSORB NUTRIENTS

Different types of roots
Huge trees in tropical forests have weak surface roots which absorb water and nutrients. Special flattened buttress roots are needed to hold the tree up (1). Plants that are tall and have a thin stem, and those that grow in mud, need special prop roots to keep them up (2). Some plants grow on trees and use clinging roots to hold on. They also have long dangling aerial roots to soak up moisture from the air (3). The first root of some young plants withers away. It is replaced by many fibrous roots (4).

ROOTS EXTEND FAR OUT FROM THE TRUNK IN THEIR SEARCH FOR WATER

Flowers

FLOWERS come in all shapes, sizes, and colours. They attract insects so that pollination occurs and seeds are produced. Plants like the lily (*right*) have large, single flowers. Others, such as the dandelion, have many tiny flowers packed together into a single flower head. Flowers have central female parts, called carpels. These consist of a stigma, style, and ovary. Each stigma is at the end of a style (stalk) and catches pollen for fertilization. The ovary contains ovules which will become seeds once fertilized. A flower's male parts are the stamens. These consist of an anther held up by a filament. Anthers produce the flower's pollen. Around these are the petals and sepals. Sepals protect a flower when it is in bud. Many flowers have special glands that secrete a sugary fluid called nectar. Nectar provides food energy for insects and is one of the rewards that plants offer in exchange for being pollinated.

WATER SUCKED UP FROM THE ROOTS FORCES THE FLOWER TO OPEN

THE TEPALS (SEPALS) PROTECT THE GROWING FLOWER

A LILY'S SEPALS LOOK LIKE PETALS AND ARE OFTEN CALLED TEPALS

WITHIN THE TIPS OF SPECIAL BRANCHES THE COMPLICATED FLOWER FORMS FROM A BUD

Flower types
Flowers come in many shapes and colours. Some are designed to attract certain insects. Poppies (1) have brightly coloured single flowers that attract bees and some flies. Many orchids (2) mimic, or copy, particular female insects, even down to their scent. The male insects try to mate with the flower and in doing so pollinate them. Dandelions (3) have large flowers made up of hundreds of tiny flowers called florets. The huge tubular flowers of the foxglove (4) attract bumble bees.

① ② ③ ④

Ovules

Inside the heart of the flower lies the next generation of plants. Here, within the female ovary, ovules develop which eventually become seeds. Each ovule consists of an egg cell, supporting tissue, and a protective coat. After fertilization the ovule swells and becomes a seed.

A CROSS-SECTION OF AN OVULE SHOWS THE EGG CELL AFTER FERTILIZATION

THE EGG-CELL WILL GROW INTO A SEED AFTER JOINING WITH A MALE CELL FROM A POLLEN GRAIN

PETALS SHOW OFF THE FLOWER AND MAKE IT ATTRACTIVE TO INSECTS

THE OVARY HOLDS THE DEVELOPING OVULES

THE STYLE SUPPORTS THE STIGMA

POLLEN LIES INSIDE THE ANTHER

A SUGARY SECRETION CALLED NECTAR IS PRODUCED TO ATTRACT INSECTS

LONG FILAMENTS SUPPORT THE ANTHERS

POLLEN GRAIN WITH WALL SURROUNDING MALE CELLS

Pollen

The anthers produce pollen grains, which will land on a visiting insect. The insect may carry them off to another lily. There, the grains may land on the stigma and fertilization will occur.

THE STIGMA RECEIVES POLLEN GRAINS WHICH GROW DOWN TO THE OVULES TO FERTILIZE THE EGG CELLS

SPECIAL MARKINGS ON THE LILY FLOWER ATTRACT INSECTS

THE ANTHER AND FILAMENT TOGETHER FORM THE STAMEN WHICH SCATTERS THE POLLEN ONTO VISITING INSECTS

INSECTS LIKE BEES CARRY POLLEN FROM FLOWER TO FLOWER, AND SO POLLINATE THEM

Pollination

FOR FERTILIZATION to occur and a seed to grow, pollen must pass from a male part of a flower (anther) to a female part (stigma). The way in which the pollen moves is called pollination. Some flowers use their own pollen. Others use pollen from the flowers of other plants of the same species. Plants use many methods to carry pollen between flowers. Grasses and some trees often use the wind. But a more efficient way is to use insects like bees, moths, flies, and beetles. Animals like the honey possum, some bats, birds and even slugs, also pollinate flowers.

After pollen has been passed on to the female stigma of a flower, the pollen develops a tube that grows down the style to an ovule. The male cell in the pollen fuses with the female egg cell in the ovule. The fertilized ovule then develops into a seed.

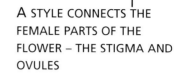

A STYLE CONNECTS THE FEMALE PARTS OF THE FLOWER – THE STIGMA AND OVULES

THE NECTARY PRODUCES SWEET NECTAR TO ATTRACT INSECTS

THE MALE ANTHERS PRODUCE MASSES OF POLLEN GRAINS

AN ANTHER DEPOSITS STICKY POLLEN ONTO THE INSECT'S BODY

POLLEN BRUSHED FROM AN INSECT'S BODY STICKS TO THE STIGMA

MALE POLLEN CELLS TRAVEL DOWN A POLLEN TUBE TO THE OVULE

CROSS POLLINATION

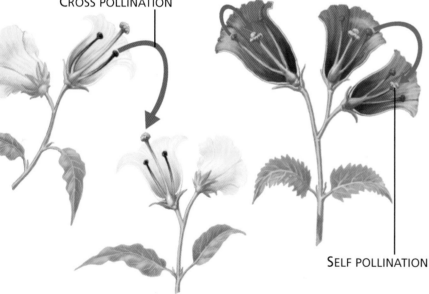

SELF POLLINATION

Types of pollination
Plants are self-pollinated when they use their own pollen to fertilize their ovules. Flowers fertilized by pollen from other plants are said to be cross-pollinated. Cross pollination is often better for a plant. It ensures that their offspring have a mix of characters from both parents. Having a mix of characters gives a better chance of survival than just having characters from a single parent.

Insect pollination
Insects attracted to flowers pick up sticky pollen on their bodies. Some flowers, like these roses, just dust the insect all over with pollen, others dab pollen on certain parts of the insect's body. Flowers are specially designed to make sure that the insect picks up pollen from the anthers, and deposits pollen from other flowers right onto the stigma. Such plants often depend upon a particular type of insect for pollination. Bees pollinate flowers as they travel from flower to flower collecting pollen to eat.

AFTER POLLINATION THE
FERTILIZED OVULE DEVELOPS
INTO A SEED

A ROSEHIP CONTAINS
SEVERAL SEEDS

A MASS OF
HOOK-LIKE
HAIRS PROTECT
THE SEEDS

A RIPE SEED READY FOR
DISPERSAL (SEE PAGES 18–19)

THE BASE OF THE STYLE

A CROSS-SECTION OF AN
OVULE

MALE POLLEN CELLS ENTER
THE OVULE

THE EGG CELL WILL FUSE
WITH THE MALE CELL FROM
THE POLLEN GRAIN – AND A
SEED WILL GROW

THE POLLEN ON THE STIGMA
PRODUCES A POLLEN TUBE
WHICH GROWS DOWN THE
STYLE TO THE OVULE

THE STYLE

Wind pollination
The male and female
parts of wind-pollinated
plants ripen at different
times so that self-
pollination does not
occur. The flowers have
feather-like stigmas to
catch the pollen grains.

Bird pollination
Humming birds reach
into flowers with their
long beaks for nectar.
Anthers dust pollen on
the bird's head. On visits
to other flowers the
pollen is transferred to
the stigma.

Mammal pollination
Some plants secrete
masses of nectar to
attract mammals like this
honey possum. Pollen
smothers the animal's
furry head as it eagerly
laps up the nectar with
its long tongue.

Seeds

SEEDS GROW into the next generation of plants. A seed develops when a plant's ovule has been fertilized (see pages 16–17). The seed then grows into an embryo, which is made up of seed leaves (cotyledons), a stem, and a root tip. Some seeds contain a store of food for the young plant to use as it begins to grow. Others store and surround themselves with food attractive to animals. The protective coating around a seed may be smooth, soft, or hard, and it may have 'wings', hairs, spines, or hooks.

Some plants live for only a year and drop their seeds around them. Others live much longer and need to spread their seeds so that the new seedlings will not grow in the soil around them, and so will not take the goodness from the soil that they themselves need. The seeds are spread, or dispersed, in many different ways.

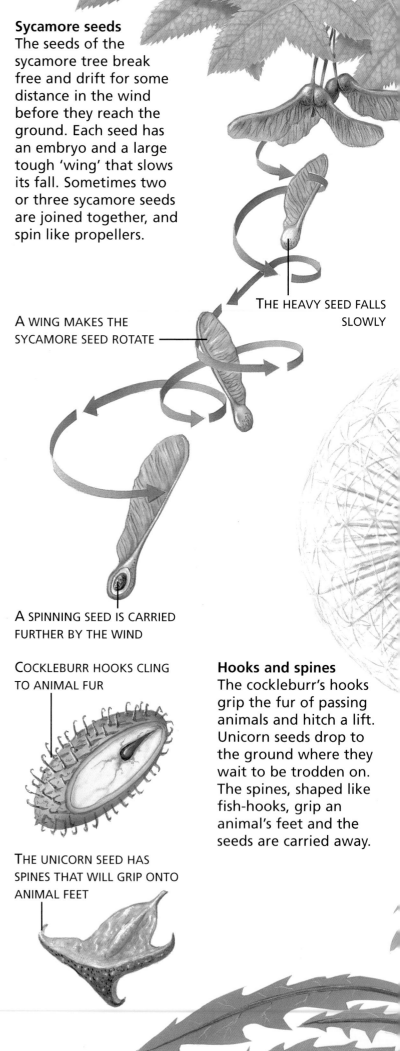

Sycamore seeds
The seeds of the sycamore tree break free and drift for some distance in the wind before they reach the ground. Each seed has an embryo and a large tough 'wing' that slows its fall. Sometimes two or three sycamore seeds are joined together, and spin like propellers.

THE HEAVY SEED FALLS SLOWLY

A WING MAKES THE SYCAMORE SEED ROTATE

A SPINNING SEED IS CARRIED FURTHER BY THE WIND

COCKLEBURR HOOKS CLING TO ANIMAL FUR

THE UNICORN SEED HAS SPINES THAT WILL GRIP ONTO ANIMAL FEET

Hooks and spines
The cockleburr's hooks grip the fur of passing animals and hitch a lift. Unicorn seeds drop to the ground where they wait to be trodden on. The spines, shaped like fish-hooks, grip an animal's feet and the seeds are carried away.

Spreading seeds
Wind, water, and animals help disperse seeds. Some seeds are specially designed to be carried by the wind. Seeds with hooks or spikes are carried away when they become attached to animal fur. Seeds inside fruits are eaten by animals, or birds like the macaw (*above*), who pass them unharmed to the ground through their droppings.

Dandelion seeds
A dandelion flower changes into a cluster of dry one-seeded fruits, called a dandelion clock. On top of each fruit is a ring of white hairs, called the pappus. After fertilization the pappus is pushed to the top of a very thin stalk. This forms the 'parachute' that lets the fruit travel many miles through the air.

THE FRUIT DANGLES ON THE END OF A LONG STALK

THE FEATHERY HAIRS FLOAT WELL IN THE BREEZE

A POPPY'S CAPSULE IS DIVIDED INTO SECTIONS

THE DANDELION CLOCK IS ON A TALL STALK AND CATCHES THE WIND

THE TINY POPPY SEEDS ARE SCATTERED BY THE WIND

PRESSURE SQUIRTS THE CUCUMBER'S SEEDS OUT

The squirting cucumber
Squirting cucumbers are explosive soft fruits (*above*). Inside the fruit hundreds of small flat seeds are stuck in a slimy mass, and surrounded by cells that are under high pressure. When ripe, the fruit is easily knocked off the plant. Its fall causes the high-pressure cells to expand, squirting the seeds out.

SEEDS ESCAPE THROUGH HOLES AROUND THE TOP

THE SEEDS ARE SHAKEN OUT OF THE HOLES

Poppy seeds
The ovaries of a poppy flower form a large fruit called a capsule. This dries out leaving the tiny seeds loose inside. Tiny holes then open around its top, letting the seeds sprinkle out like salt from a salt-cellar.

SOME PLANTS PRODUCE EDIBLE FRUITS – SEEDS INSIDE THESE ARE UNHARMED WHEN EATEN BY THE ANIMAL

Apples
The petals, stamens, and five ovaries of the apple flower are fixed to a piece of tissue called the receptacle. When the seeds are fertilized this swells and surrounds them, forming a thick, fleshy fruit.

Hazel nuts
Each nut is a dry fruit containing a seed (the kernel), with a hard, protective ovary wall. Some animals store nuts for winter. Sometimes they forget where they have put them and the nuts germinate and grow.

Blackberries
Each blackberry is made of fruitlets called drupels. The thick ovary wall surrounding the seed is sweet and full of sugar. The seeds, protected by tough outer coats, are eaten by animals and dispersed in their droppings.

New Growth

I N THE RIGHT conditions, seeds begin to grow into new plants in a process called germination. In autumn, bean seeds (*below*) drop from the shrivelled pods of adult plants. Some become buried, while others are eaten or taken away by animals. In spring, the sun warms the soil, and the embryo plant inside the seed comes to life. The seed absorbs water and begins to swell up. Then the embryo starts to grow using food stored in the seed's special fleshy leaves. In a few days, out pops the first root, which grows down, and the first shoot, which grows up.

Seeds are not the only source of new growth. Like seeds, spores also grow into new plants (*see page 22*). Stems, shoots, and roots form new plants too, but in a different way (*above*).

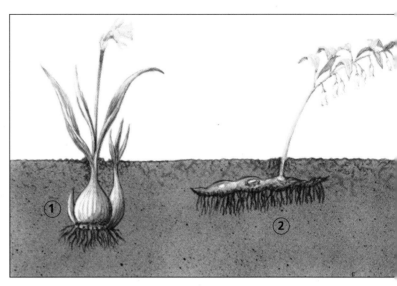

Growth without seeds
Daffodil bulbs are short swollen underground shoots (1). Each has a short stem at its centre, surrounded by fleshy scales that contain food for new plant growth. In spring, buds grow from the bulb and produce roots, flowers, and leaves.

Underground stems, like those of Solomon's seal, grow near the soil surface (2). These are called rhizomes. New leaves, buds, and roots grow from them, spreading new plants across the surrounding area. Hidden and protected underground,

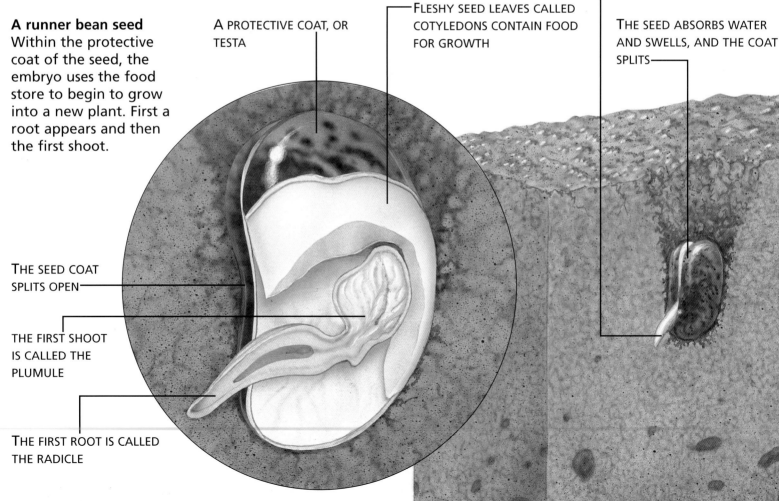

A runner bean seed
Within the protective coat of the seed, the embryo uses the food store to begin to grow into a new plant. First a root appears and then the first shoot.

A PROTECTIVE COAT, OR TESTA

FLESHY SEED LEAVES CALLED COTYLEDONS CONTAIN FOOD FOR GROWTH

THE RADICLE EMERGES AS THE EMBRYO GROWS

THE SEED ABSORBS WATER AND SWELLS, AND THE COAT SPLITS

THE SEED COAT SPLITS OPEN

THE FIRST SHOOT IS CALLED THE PLUMULE

THE FIRST ROOT IS CALLED THE RADICLE

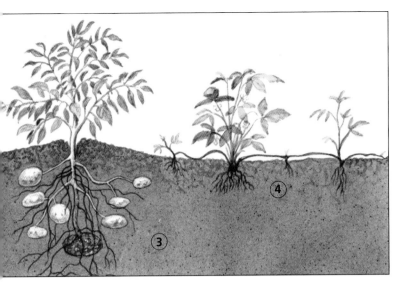

THE TOP SHOOT WITH NEW LEAVES COILS AROUND A SUPPORTING CANE

A SHIELD BUG SUCKS SAP FROM A LEAF

THE SHRIVELLED REMAINS OF THE SEED LEAVES

THE FIRST REAL LEAVES OPEN AND THE PLANT STARTS TO GROW FASTER

they help the plants to survive in the winter. Thin underground stems grow from near the lower leaves of potato plants (3). These branch and swell into tubers which store food and grow into new potato plants the following year.

THE PLUMULE BREAKS OUT OF THE SEED COAT AND HEADS UPWARDS, AWAY FROM THE DOWNWARD —FORCE OF GRAVITY

THE RADICLE GROWS DOWN, GROWING INTO NEW ROOTS

Strawberry plants produce special shoots called runners near the soil surface (4). Buds grow at intervals along them. Where the buds touch the soil, roots grow, and a new plant forms.

THE ROOT GROWS AND THE SEED LEAVES WITHER AS THEIR FOOD STORE IS USED

Spores

SOME PLANTS, such as mosses, ferns, and conifers, produce spores instead of seeds. Spores are like seeds, but much smaller and simpler. For spores to develop on a moss plant, the plant must produce male gametes (sperm) and female gametes (eggs). Eggs fertilized by the sperm grow while still fixed to the moss plant. At this stage the spores, which grow into other moss plants, are produced. Mosses have simple leaves and a stem, but no roots. They have no vessels to transport water and so are unable to grow taller than 20 centimetres.

Ferns are more complicated, with roots, leaves (fronds), and stems containing vessels that carry water throughout the plant. Spores grow on the underside of the fronds. They fall to the ground and develop into tiny green plants which produce eggs or sperm. The fertilized eggs grow into new fern plants.

Ferns
Like mosses, ferns produce spores and male and female gametes (sperm and eggs). But unlike mosses, the spores and gametes are produced on separate plants called gametophytes.

Ferns like the delicate lady fern (*below*) must live in a damp or wet place because its sperm have to swim to find the eggs.

ON THE UNDERSIDE OF THE FROND SPORES GROW IN TINY CASES CALLED SPORANGIA

Mosses
While still fixed to the plant, a moss plant's fertilized eggs produce capsules in which spores are formed. When the spores are ready, the capsules' lids fall off. As the capsules dry, special teeth bend back, letting the spores escape. Tiny hairs inside the capsules dry too, twist and turn, and force the spores out. Gusts of wind help carry them away. On damp ground they grow into new moss plants.

A FERN'S FROND UNCOILS AS IT GROWS

SPECIAL TEETH BEND OUT TO RELEASE THE THE SPORES

YOUNG FRONDS ARE COILED UP

SPORANGIA OFTEN GROW IN GROUPS

A fern's spores
Spores grow in cases, called sporangia, on the underside of the fronds. Sporangia occur in groups, protected beneath a fold of tissue. When ripe, the spores are flicked out as the walls of the sporangia dry. The spores drift on the wind and germinate (begin to grow) after landing on damp ground.

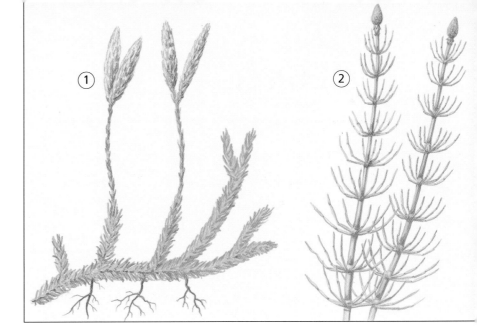

A CROSS-SECTION OF A FROND AND SPORANGIUM

SPORES FORM IN THE SPORANGIUM

SPORES ARE BLOWN AWAY BY THE WIND

Ferns' relatives
Hundreds of millions of years ago clubmosses grew tall and tree-like. Their remains became coal. Today, clubmosses are small plants with roots and a stem densely covered in tiny leaves (1). Clubmosses were the first plants to produce their reproductive parts in cones.

Growing alongside the ancient clubmosses were huge forests of giant horsetails. Today, they do not grow as tall (2 metres at most). Their ridged stems have long thin leaves arranged in rings (2). Both club-mosses and horsetails live in damp places.

A SPORE GERMINATES AND GROWS INTO A TINY FERN PLANT CALLED A GAMETOPHYTE

THE TINY PLANT PRODUCES EITHER MALE SPERM OR FEMALE EGGS

A FEMALE PLANT GROWS EGGS IN A SPECIAL CUP

A MALE PLANT PRODUCES SPERM

SPERM SWIM IN MOISTURE TO FIND AN EGG

A FERN'S UNDERGROUND STEM CAN ALSO GROW INTO NEW FERN PLANTS

THE SPERM JOINS WITH AN EGG

A FERTILIZED EGG GROWS INTO A NEW SPORE-PRODUCING FERN

A YOUNG FERN'S ROOTS GROW DOWN AND ITS TINY STEM AND LEAVES GROW UP

Trees

TREES ARE the largest land plants, growing to over 40 metres in height. Trees can grow this tall because they are made of wood. The wood makes them very strong, but also flexible so that they bend rather than break in the wind. An outer skin of thick dead cells, called the bark, and a layer of dead, spongy cells, called cork, protect the tree. Beneath these are storage tissue and bundles of vessels (tubes), called the phloem, which carry food throughout the plant. Next to the phloem is the cambium – a very thin layer of cells. This is the growing layer of the tree which produces phloem on its outside and live sapwood on its inside. The sapwood contains fibres of strong, thicker cells, and long xylem vessels which carry water up the tree. As the tree grows, the inner sapwood dies and is changed into strong heartwood. In dry or cold weather, growth is slower. This results in a series of annual growth rings.

BUDS OPEN IN SPRING

THE TREE GROWS IN SUMMER

LEAVES FALL IN AUTUMN

THE TREE RESTS IN WINTER

Bark beetles
The bark beetle burrows into the wood behind the bark. Females chew a main tunnel with side galleries in which they lay their eggs. The larvae eat the live tissue and fungi that grow beneath the bark.

AN ASH BARK BEETLE

BARK BEETLE GALLERIES FORM DISTINCTIVE PATTERNS

Deciduous trees
The changing seasons throughout the year affect the growth of a deciduous tree. Winter is a time to rest, with no leaves and little or no growth. In spring the buds open, producing leaves and flowers. During spring and summer the leaves make food for the growing tree. The flowers provide seeds and fruit.

LARGE VESSELS GROW IN THE SPRING AND SUMMER WHEN THE WEATHER IS WARM AND FOOD IS MORE PLENTIFUL

GROWTH RINGS VARY ACCORDING TO CONDITIONS – NARROW RINGS INDICATE SLOW GROWTH DURING PARTICULARLY DRY YEARS

In autumn nutrients and chlorophyll (the green colouring) in the leaves are removed and stored for the following year. The leaves are then sealed off from their water supply causing them to shrivel, die, and fall.

THE XYLEM VESSELS OF THE SAPWOOD CARRY WATER AND SALTS UP THE TREE

THE DEAD HEARTWOOD FORMS THE INNER WOOD AND IS SPECIALLY HARDENED FOR STRENGTH

Food paths

Tiny root hairs absorb water as well as minerals from the soil. Sugars and other foods made by the leaves are carried to the rest of the tree inside the phloem. As water evaporates through the leaves it is drawn up from the roots and carried throughout the tree in the xylem vessels.

WATER IS USED TO MAKE FOOD (PHOTOSYNTHESIS) AND TO TRANSPORT IT AROUND THE TREE

WATER AND NUTRIENTS TRAVEL UP THE TREE; SUGARS AND FOOD TRAVEL DOWN

THE ROOTS ABSORB WATER AND MINERAL NUTRIENTS FROM THE SOIL AND RECEIVE FOODS FROM THE LEAVES

THE PROTECTIVE BARK IS FORMED FROM DEAD CELLS

THE INNER BARK IS SOFT AND SPONGY AND FORMS CORK

A LAYER OF PHLOEM VESSELS AND STORAGE TISSUES GROW OUT FROM THE CAMBIUM

LARGE SUMMER AND SMALL AUTUMN VESSELS TOGETHER MAKE A GROWTH RING

THE THIN CAMBIUM IS THE GROWING LAYER OF THE TREE

LARGE XYLEM VESSEL OF EARLY (SPRING) WOOD

FOOD IS STORED IN SPECIAL STRANDS THAT LIE ACROSS THE GROWTH RINGS IN THE SAPWOOD

Wood structure

Wood is formed from a mass of vessels that carry water and nutrients up the tree. These are supported by strong, fine fibres. Vessels produced in the spring and summer are much larger than those in the autumn. Between the vessels food storage cells form strands, called rays, at right angles to the growth rings.

SMALL VESSEL OF LATE (AUTUMN) WOOD

LARGE BANDS OF STORAGE TISSUE

LICHENS (PLANTS WHICH ARE PART FUNGI AND PART ALGAE) GROW ON THE BARK

Conifers

UNLIKE DECIDUOUS trees, conifers do not produce flowers. Instead of flowers, they have cones. Male cones make pollen which is then carried by the wind to female cones. The pollen fertilizes the female cone's ovules, which develop into seeds.

Many conifers grow in places that are too cold or dry for other trees. Conifer seeds are very tough so they can withstand the intense winter cold. The trees themselves have needle-like leaves which greatly reduces water-loss. This is especially important in winter, when the soil is frozen and water is unavailable. They also have resins and oils in their wood which seal any injuries and protect the tree against the cold.

In the regions where conifers grow, the summers are short so the trees grow very fast. Huge forests of conifers occur across northern Europe, Asia, and Canada.

Corsican pine
Unlike many pines, the Corsican pine originally grew in warm, dry areas (in Corsica and southern Italy). It is now very common everywhere – in parks, gardens, and in large forests on poor, sandy soils. It grows to over 40 metres and has greenish-grey leaves.

SLOPING BRANCHES ENABLE SNOW TO FALL OFF EASILY

BRANCHES ARE LONGER LOWER DOWN THE TRUNK – FOR STABILITY AND SO THAT THEY CAN GATHER SUNLIGHT

FAST-GROWING, STRAIGHT TRUNK

Pine needles
Because they live in dry places conifers need special leaves. Plants usually lose water through stomata on the surface of their leaves. The leaves of conifers are long and narrow, so less water can escape. To protect the stomata the leaves are rolled with the stomata tucked in the fold. The leaves are also covered in a thick, waxy waterproof 'skin'.

CHANNEL FOR TRANSPORTING RESIN (A STICKY, OILY FLUID)

STOMA PROTECTED IN A SUNKEN PIT

TOUGH, WAXY 'SKIN'

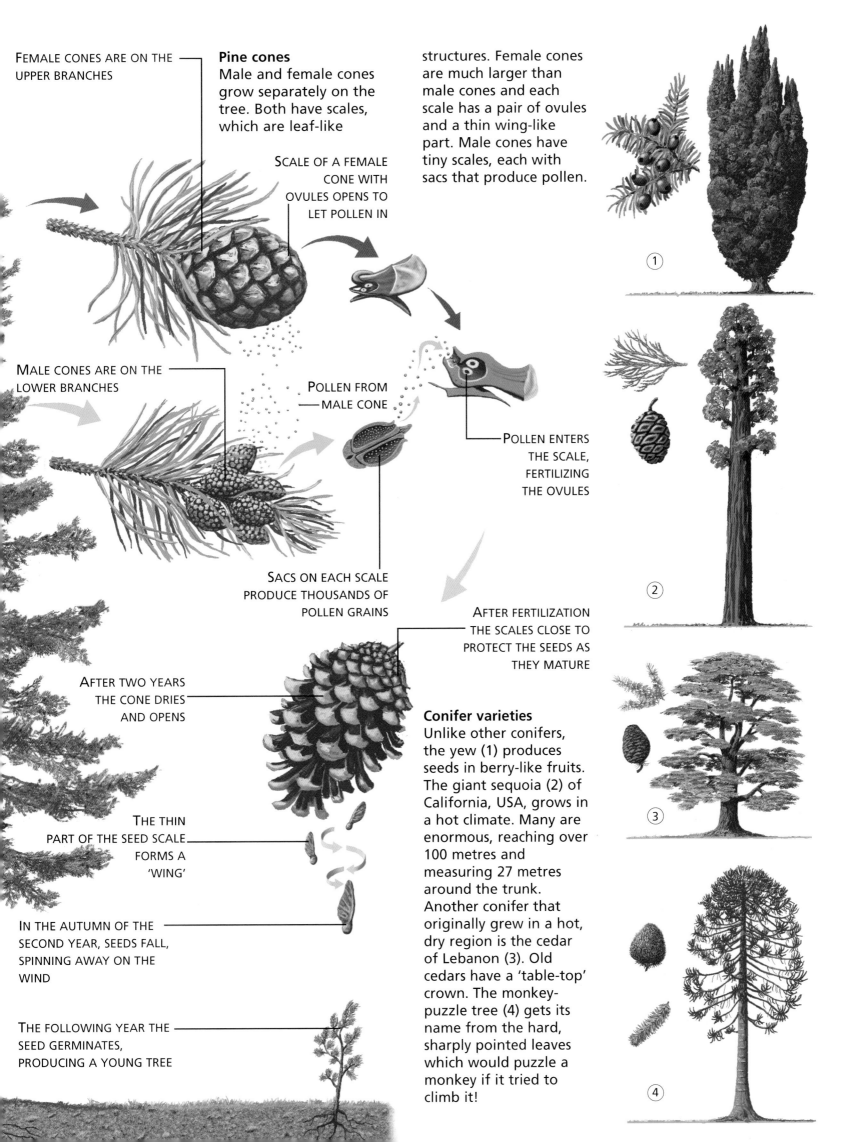

FEMALE CONES ARE ON THE UPPER BRANCHES

Pine cones
Male and female cones grow separately on the tree. Both have scales, which are leaf-like

SCALE OF A FEMALE CONE WITH OVULES OPENS TO LET POLLEN IN

structures. Female cones are much larger than male cones and each scale has a pair of ovules and a thin wing-like part. Male cones have tiny scales, each with sacs that produce pollen.

MALE CONES ARE ON THE LOWER BRANCHES

POLLEN FROM MALE CONE

POLLEN ENTERS THE SCALE, FERTILIZING THE OVULES

SACS ON EACH SCALE PRODUCE THOUSANDS OF POLLEN GRAINS

AFTER FERTILIZATION THE SCALES CLOSE TO PROTECT THE SEEDS AS THEY MATURE

AFTER TWO YEARS THE CONE DRIES AND OPENS

Conifer varieties
Unlike other conifers, the yew (1) produces seeds in berry-like fruits. The giant sequoia (2) of California, USA, grows in a hot climate. Many are enormous, reaching over 100 metres and measuring 27 metres around the trunk. Another conifer that originally grew in a hot, dry region is the cedar of Lebanon (3). Old cedars have a 'table-top' crown. The monkey-puzzle tree (4) gets its name from the hard, sharply pointed leaves which would puzzle a monkey if it tried to climb it!

THE THIN PART OF THE SEED SCALE FORMS A 'WING'

IN THE AUTUMN OF THE SECOND YEAR, SEEDS FALL, SPINNING AWAY ON THE WIND

THE FOLLOWING YEAR THE SEED GERMINATES, PRODUCING A YOUNG TREE

Desert Plants

PLANTS THAT live in deserts have to put up with extremely dry conditions and often great changes in temperature. However, a wide variety of plants live here, each using different ways to survive in the hostile climate. Many are succulent. This means they hold the water that reaches them, either in their leaves, their stems, or their roots. Some avoid water-loss by having no leaves at all, or by having waterproof or thin leaves which can easily be shed in a drought. The stomata are often hidden deep in pits. The leaves may even reflect the sun's heat or prevent damage from frost at night. Their flowers may be quite large, relying not so much on insects but on birds and bats to pollinate them. Tough coats protect their seeds during long periods of drought. When rain falls or floods rise they quickly germinate and grow.

THE WHITE PETALS ATTRACT BIRDS FOR POLLINATION

Flowering cactus
The flowers of some cacti, like this saguaro, open during the day, but many cacti flowers open at night. They are often large and extremely beautiful. They attract large moths, bats and birds, which pollinate them.

SIDE SHOOT WITH FLOWER BUDS

Plant types
The dense rosette of succulent agave leaves (1) have special tissues for storing water. Fibres from the leaves are sometimes used to make string. The masses of spines covering the bushy opuntia (2) protect it against grazing animals and reflect the sun's heat. Echinocerus (3) is well-adapted to the desert and has no leaves. Its ridged stem can expand to store water.

The common prickly pear cactus (4) forms dense prickly scrub. This American cactus has been introduced into other parts of the world and has grown so well it has become a plague.

SAND PILES UP ON THE WINDWARD SIDE

ROOTS GATHER RARE AND VALUABLE WATER FROM RAIN AND DEW

THE ELF OWL MAKES ITS
NEST IN HOLES IN THE
LIVING CACTUS

IN THE HOLE, CHICKS ARE
PROTECTED FROM THE
HEAT OF THE SUN

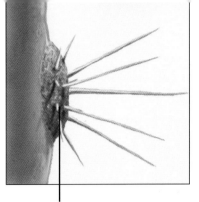

TUFTS OF SPINES PROTECT
THE PLANT FROM GRAZING
ANIMALS AND REFLECT THE
SUN'S HEAT AWAY

CACTUS SKIN HAS A THICK
WAXY LAYER FOR
WATERPROOFING

HARD, WOODY TISSUE
CARRIES WATER THROUGH-
OUT THE PLANT

LONG FIBROUS ROOTS SEEK
OUT NUTRIENTS JUST
BENEATH THE SOIL SURFACE

SOFT STEM TISSUE
CARRIES SUGARY FOODS

STOMATA

A THICK LAYER OF LARGE
CELLS STORES WATER

A THICK MASS
OF FIBROUS ROOTS
ANCHORS THE PLANT

Inside cacti

In cacti the stomata,
which all plants need for
the exchange of carbon
dioxide and oxygen, are
sunk deep inside pits to
reduce water-loss. Large
cells form a thick, soft
layer for storing water.
Soft tissues deep within
the stem carry water and
nutrients throughout
the plant.

Wetland Plants

THERE ARE many kinds of wetlands, including salty coastal waters, muddy swamps and marshes, freshwater lakeshores and ponds, and fast-flowing rivers. They provide many different habitats where plants can live, from water-logged soils to sunlit surface waters.

A pond that gets plenty of sunshine (*right*) can provide all that a plant needs, including nutrients and support. However, living in water has its problems. Oxygen and carbon dioxide may be in short supply, so some plants have special air-carrying tissue. Light may not reach the bottom of a pond, so many plants must float near the surface. The water and its surface provide support for plants. Some water plants have leaves and flowers that rest on the surface, while their flimsy stems are supported by the water below.

Water lilies

The anchoring roots of water lilies form food-storing tubers. Other water plants have roots that dangle in the water, absorbing nutrients. Water lily flowers attract insects during the day, and then close at night, trapping them. During the night the insects pollinate the ovules. In the morning the flowers open again, releasing their guests.

REEDS AND OTHER MARSH PLANTS GROW IN THE WATER-LOGGED SOIL

PLANTS LIKE BULRUSHES HAVE SPECIAL STEMS TO TAKE OXYGEN DOWN TO THEIR SUBMERGED ROOTS

WATER LILY FLOWERS AND LEAVES REST ON THE SURFACE OF THE WATER

Algae

Surrounded by nutrients, many microscopic plants, called algae, grow freely in the water or attach themselves to other plants or rocks. Many algae are made of single cells or groups of cells. Spirogyra, also known as blanket weed (*right*), forms dense tangled mats, providing homes to many other tiny algae and animals.

SPIROGYRA (VIEWED THROUGH A MICROSCOPE)

BARE SURFACES, LIKE ROCKS, BECOME COVERED IN ALGAE

THE ROOTS OF SOME WATER PLANTS HOLD THEM FIRMLY IN THE MUD

THE TINY FLOWERS ON A
BULRUSH ARE PACKED INTO
THESE SAUSAGE SHAPES

TALL PLANTS GROWING ON
THE EDGE OF THE POND HAVE
STRONG ANCHOR ROOTS

DUCKWEEDS HAVE NO
STEM – THEY ARE THE
SMALLEST FLOWERING
PLANTS

Ribbon-weed
The tropical ribbon-weed
(*below right*) uses the
water for pollination.
Male flower buds
develop and are released
(1). They float to the
surface, open, and sail
across to a female flower
(2). The female flower
opens on the surface to
reveal its stigma (3).
Once fertilized by
a male bud, the
female stalk spirals
down (4), pulling the
fertilized ovule to
the bottom, where
the seeds are released.

THE WATER SOLDIER
RESTS ON THE BOTTOM
UNTIL LATE SPRING,
THEN RISES TO THE
SURFACE AND
FLOWERS

HORSETAILS HAVE HOLLOW
STEMS THAT EXTEND VERY
DEEP INTO THE SOIL

Ocean Plants

FLOWERING sea grasses and simple non-flowering algae live in the oceans. Most ocean plants are tiny algae called phytoplankton, which live near the surface. Many larger species of algae (seaweeds) live in cool, shallow coastal waters and on seashores. Like all plants, algae need sunlight for photosynthesis, so cannot live deeper than 175 metres where sunlight does not reach.

Seaweeds do not have vascular tissue (xylem and phloem), or proper leaves, roots, or stems. The larger ones grow as delicate tufts, flat sheets, and thick fronds. Some are over a hundred metres long. They reproduce by growing spores which join in the open sea to form new plants. Seaweeds are classified according to their colour. Brown and most green seaweeds need direct sunlight, so live in shallow water. Many red seaweeds and a few greens need only a little light and are found in deeper waters.

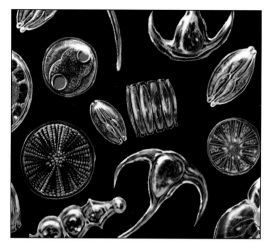

Phytoplankton
Microscopic phytoplankton live in the top few metres of cooler seas. They can be very abundant (a mouthful of seawater may contain 30 million)! Phytoplankton are very important as they produce much of the oxygen we breathe. They also provide food for tiny animals and form the beginning of the marine food chain.

TOUGH FRONDS CAN WITHSTAND THE BATTERING OF THE SURF

AIR-FILLED BLADDER

Types of seaweed
Sea sorrel (1) is a green seaweed that lives on rocks in shallow pools. It has a disc-like holdfast and feathery branched stem. Sugar kelp (2) is a large brown seaweed, so-called because it is sweet and edible. The greatest variety of seaweeds are red. Calliblepharis (3) has a leafy frond. It is an annual plant (lives for a year), unlike sugar kelp which is a perennial (lives for several years). Not all seaweeds are leafy, strap-like, or feathery. The brown seaweed, ralfsia, forms irregular lumps on exposed rocks (4).

THE FRONDS ARE UNCOVERED WHEN THE TIDE GOES OUT

THE TOUGH FRONDS WITHSTAND DRYING OUT BECAUSE THEY CONTAIN SPECIAL SLIME THAT PROTECTS THEIR CELLS

Life around a seaweed
The seaweed itself, especially its holdfast, provides a safe home for many animals. Some, such as crabs, leave their safe retreat to feed in the open. Others, such as various limpets, eat the seaweed.

SUNLIGHT PENETRATES
THE SEA DOWN TO ABOUT
175 METRES

Reproduction

The seaweed on the left is called bladder wrack. It has eggs and sperm which are produced inside special cavities called conceptacles. These are located at the tips of the fronds. They release the sperm and eggs into the sea where they fuse and settle on rocks to grow into new seaweed plants.

BLADDERS KEEP FRONDS
AFLOAT SO THAT THEY
CAN REACH AS MUCH
LIGHT AS POSSIBLE

RIPENING FEMALE EGG

JELLY-LIKE INTERIOR

CONCEPTACLES PRODUCE
EGGS AND SPERM

MALE SPERM
ARE RELEASED

Agar jelly

A jelly called agar is extracted from the jelly plant (*right*). This is used in the drug industry for growing bacteria. It is also added to many foods, such as canned food and ice-cream as a gelling agent. Dentists also use it to take impressions of teeth.

THE STRONG STIPE (STEM) IS
FLEXIBLE

SEAWEED HAS A ROOT-LIKE
HOLDFAST WHICH FIRMLY
ANCHORS THE PLANT TO A
ROCK

SPONGE

LIMPET

CRAB

Carnivores

THERE ARE about 550 species of plants from all over the world that are carnivorous, which means meat-eating. They live in places where there is little food in the soil, so they need extra food. They attract, trap, and digest insects, spiders, small animals such as lizards, and even small mammals. The way they trap these creatures varies. Some, like the sundew plant, have sticky hairs to hold their prey, while the Venus flytrap uses its leaves as spring-loaded 'jaws'. The pitcher plant (*right*) lures its victims into a slippery jug filled with a liquid that drowns them and helps the plant to digest them. All carnivorous plants use enzymes (chemicals) to dissolve their victims, and have special cells that absorb the food, which is then transported around the plant to help it grow.

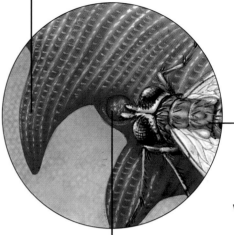

THE SPECIAL LEAVES OF A PITCHER PLANT SPROUT FROM THE STEM AND ARE LEAF-LIKE FOR PART OF THEIR LENGTH

PERISTOMES (TEETH-LIKE STRUCTURES) COATED IN SLIPPERY WAX POINT DOWNWARD

INSECT SLIPS AND FALLS WHILE TRYING TO REACH NECTAR

THE NECTAR GLAND MAKES A SWEET LIQUID TO ATTRACT INSECTS

A STRONG SPRINGY TENDRIL SUPPORTS THE PITCHER

Slippery edge
Wax makes the edge of the pitcher very slippery (*above*). Insects lured by the nectar cannot grip the surface. They slip, fall, and drown in the liquid.

THE SPIRAL GIVES THE PLANT MORE HOLD ON NEIGHBOURING PLANTS

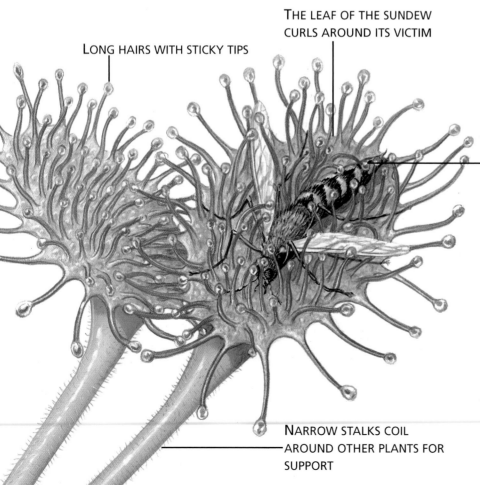

THE LEAF OF THE SUNDEW CURLS AROUND ITS VICTIM

LONG HAIRS WITH STICKY TIPS

THE INSECT IS STUCK, TRAPPED BY STICKY HAIRS

Sundew
Long hairs tipped with a sweet and sticky substance cover the leaves of the sundew. An insect may be attracted to the sweetness and settle to feed, or it may land on the leaves to rest. It soon gets stuck to the hairs, and as it struggles it gets more stuck. The plant's enzymes (digestive juices) then dissolve the insect into a liquid, which the plant absorbs.

FLUID IS DRAWN UP INTO THE PLANT

NUTRIENT FLUID IS TAKEN UP IN LEAF TUBES

NARROW STALKS COIL AROUND OTHER PLANTS FOR SUPPORT

TRIGGER BRISTLES CLOSE THE TRAP IF TOUCHED BY AN INSECT

NECTAR GLANDS ATTRACT INSECT

A FLY LANDS ON THE PAD

THE LID CREATES A SHADOW WHICH HELPS LURE INSECTS IN AND KEEPS TROPICAL RAINS OUT

A FLY IS ATTRACTED TO THE NECTAR

THE FLY TOUCHES TRIGGER HAIRS

ONCE TRIGGER HAIRS ARE TOUCHED, THE TRAP STARTS TO CLOSE

THE RIBBED RIM PROVIDES A LANDING PLATFORM FOR INSECTS

THE TRAP CLOSES – THERE IS NO ESCAPE FOR THE INSECT AS SPINES ALONG THE TRAP'S EDGE FORM A CAGE

THE INNER SURFACE OF THE PITCHER IS WAXY AND VERY SLIPPERY

THE FLY IS SLOWLY DIGESTED IN THE TRAP

ONCE AN INSECT FALLS INTO THE POND IT CANNOT GET OUT

Venus flytrap

When an insect lands on the lobes of the Venus flytrap's leaf, it touches fine trigger hairs that cause the trap to shut. As the insect struggles, the trap tightens. The plant secretes water and digestive enzymes into the trap, drowning and dissolving the insect.

GLANDS PRODUCE DIGESTIVE ENZYMES

ENZYMES SECRETED INTO THE POND DISSOLVE THE INSECTS SO THE FOOD IS IN A FORM THAT THE PLANT CAN DIGEST

REMAINS OF INSECTS

Parasitic Plants

SOME FLOWERING plants lack chlorophyll and so cannot make their own food. Plants like cytinus (see *right*) and the giant flowering rafflesia are called parasites and rely on other plants, their hosts, for their food. Half-parasites, such as mistletoe, contain chlorophyll which makes food for the plants, but as they live away from the soil they depend on their hosts for water and minerals.

Most parasitic plants cling to their host and invade its tissues using suckers, called haustoria. These root-like organs connect with the host's vascular tissue, through which the host's nutrients are flowing. The parasite taps onto and takes the nutrients, like a vampire sucking blood. Some parasites, such as rafflesia, are almost hidden inside the host, only emerging to flower. Others, such as mistletoe, grow mainly on the outside of their host.

CYTINUS HAS NO CHLOROPHYLL AND SO CANNOT PHOTOSYNTHESIZE FOOD

IN THE SUMMER A TIGHT MASS OF FLOWERS GROWS

BRACTS SURROUND AND PROTECT THE DELICATE FLOWERS

BRACTS ARE LEAF-LIKE STRUCTURES

THE PARASITE INVADES THE ROOT OF THE HOST

How it feeds

The parasite cytinus detects chemicals on the surface of a shrub, which show that it is a suitable host. It grows a patch of tissue over the host's root. From this patch, root-like haustoria burrow in. Strands of xylem and phloem in the haustoria make a connection from the vascular tissue of the parasite to that of the host.

ROOT OF THE HOST PLANT

HAUSTORIA GROW INTO THE ROOT OF THE HOST AND DRAW UP THE HOST'S NUTRIENTS

VASCULAR TISSUE FROM THE PARASITE JOINS THE HOST'S XYLEM AND PHLOEM

THE BRIGHT, COLOURFUL
FLOWERS ATTRACT INSECTS
FOR POLLINATION

THE PARASITE GROWS A
PATCH OF TISSUE AROUND
THE ROOT OF THE HOST

THE HOST'S
ROOT

WHEN NOT IN FLOWER
CYTINUS IS ONLY VISIBLE AS
A LUMP OF TISSUE ON THE
HOST'S ROOT

PHLOEM AND XYLEM FORM
THE VASCULAR TISSUE OF
THE HOST

HAUSTORIA PENETRATE INTO
THE HOST'S XYLEM

Mistletoe

Unlike other parasites,
the evergreen leaves of
the mistletoe produce
food for the plant. But
its haustoria join the
host's xylem in order to
get water and minerals,
taken from the
soil by the
host's roots.

Balanophores

Parasites called
balanophores have
strange flowers. These
parasites infect the roots
of tropical trees. The
seeds settle on the roots
and grow large tubers.
These penetrate the
host's roots.

Rafflesia

This parasite grows almost
entirely in its host's roots.
Its flowers, the biggest in
the world (up to 1.5
metres across), burst from
the roots. They smell
awful but rodents like to
eat the berries. Its seeds
are carried to new hosts
in the rodent's droppings.

Fungi

FUNGI ARE not classed as plants. Although some look like plants, they are quite different. Unlike most plants they do not contain chlorophyll and cannot make their own food. Instead, fungi feed on dead and living animal and plant material. The honey fungus (*see right*) feeds on the wood of both living and dead trees.

The main part of a fungus is called the mycelium. It is made up of a mass of delicate, thread-like tubes called hyphae. The reproductive parts of fungi are called fruiting bodies. A great variety of fruiting bodies are produced by different types of fungus, from tiny balls on stalks to large mushrooms that people like to eat.

Spores

To reproduce, fungi use spores. Many larger fungi produce their spores on the surface of plates called gills. These dangle beneath the cap and are arranged like the spokes of a wheel. Special club-shaped cells on the surface of the gills, the basidia, produce spores on the ends of tiny fingers. A single basidium usually produces four spores, but sometimes two or eight.

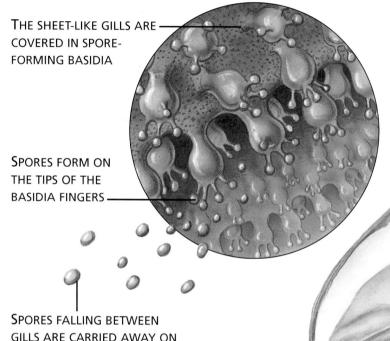

THE SHEET-LIKE GILLS ARE COVERED IN SPORE-FORMING BASIDIA

SPORES FORM ON THE TIPS OF THE BASIDIA FINGERS

SPORES FALLING BETWEEN GILLS ARE CARRIED AWAY ON THE WIND

THE OUTER SKIN OF THE STIPE (STALK)

THE FLESHY STIPE IS MADE OF MYCELIUM

AS THE MUSHROOM AGES THE GILLS DARKEN

THE WIND OR FALLING RAINDROPS FORCE THE SPORES OUT

THE SPORES ARE CARRIED INTO THE AIR

MASSES OF SPORES FORM IN THE THICK WHITE FLESH OF THE FRUITING BODY

The giant puff-ball

The fruiting body of the giant puff-ball (*left*) is a thick fleshy white mass where special cells produce spores. Slowly the cells die and the white flesh dries up. The spores are left behind inside the now dry, papery shell. The touch of a raindrop or breeze forces the tiny spores out.

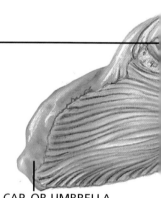

THE CAP, OR UMBRELLA, FLATTENS AND MAY CURL AT THE EDGES

A YOUNG MUSHROOM DEVELOPS AS A 'BUTTON' OF DENSE MYCELIUM

THE DENSE MYCELIUM FORMS A ROOT-LIKE MASS

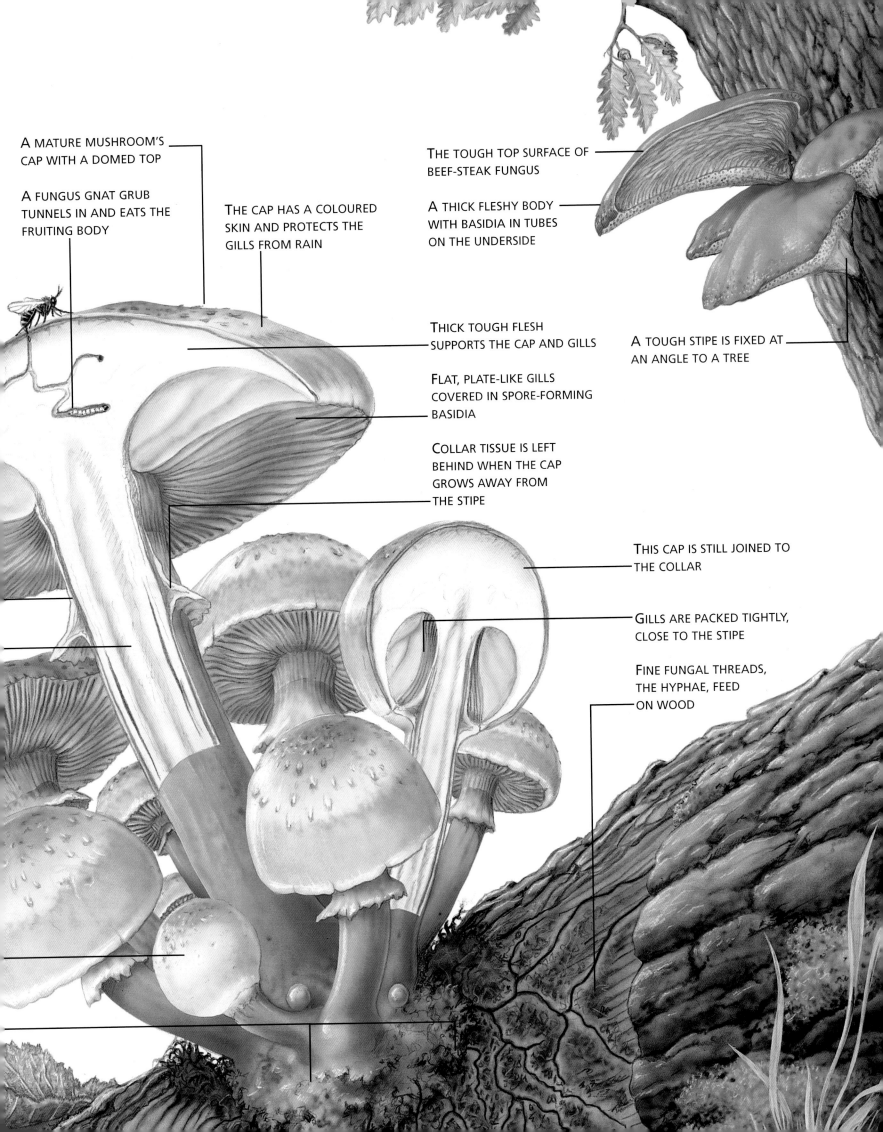

A MATURE MUSHROOM'S CAP WITH A DOMED TOP

A FUNGUS GNAT GRUB TUNNELS IN AND EATS THE FRUITING BODY

THE CAP HAS A COLOURED SKIN AND PROTECTS THE GILLS FROM RAIN

THE TOUGH TOP SURFACE OF BEEF-STEAK FUNGUS

A THICK FLESHY BODY WITH BASIDIA IN TUBES ON THE UNDERSIDE

THICK TOUGH FLESH SUPPORTS THE CAP AND GILLS

A TOUGH STIPE IS FIXED AT AN ANGLE TO A TREE

FLAT, PLATE-LIKE GILLS COVERED IN SPORE-FORMING BASIDIA

COLLAR TISSUE IS LEFT BEHIND WHEN THE CAP GROWS AWAY FROM THE STIPE

THIS CAP IS STILL JOINED TO THE COLLAR

GILLS ARE PACKED TIGHTLY, CLOSE TO THE STIPE

FINE FUNGAL THREADS, THE HYPHAE, FEED ON WOOD

Rainforest

TROPICAL rainforest provides perfect growing conditions for plants. As many as 700 different kinds of tree grow in a single area. Most grow over 50 metres tall. The animal life is as rich as the plant life, and the two depend upon each other.

The rainforest is divided into layers. From the air it looks like a green ocean. This is the canopy, the top layer, where the trees expose their crowns to the sun. Most of the rainforest animals are found in this crowded layer. Beneath the canopy, young trees form an understorey layer. If a tree falls, light breaks through the canopy, and young understorey trees quickly grow to fill the space. Vines and creepers also climb to reach the light. Orchids, ferns, and bromeliad plants grow on branches. In the lowest layer of the forest there is almost no sunlight and few plants can grow.

THE CANOPY IS THE BRIGHTEST, WARMEST, AND WETTEST LAYER

VERY TALL TREES EMERGE ABOVE THE CANOPY

THE SOIL IS THIN AND FULL OF FINE TREE ROOTS, WHICH QUICKLY ABSORB THE NUTRIENTS

Bromeliads
Bromeliads are epiphytes – plants that grow on others without harming them. They rely on trees to lift them from the darkness of the forest floor. Bromeliads' cup-like leaves trap water which would other-wise run down to the ground.

FROGS AND INSECTS LIVE IN THE WATER IN BROMELIADS

Ant plants
Ant plants have a swollen stem that provides ants with a safe home to live in. The ants help the plant in return by defending it against attack from other insects. Also, the ants' droppings give the plant extra nutrients for growth.

THE ANT PLANT'S HOST TREE

NEST IN SWOLLEN STEM

Rainforest life
The tall trees of the canopy provide timber for building and furniture. When a tree falls it tears an opening in the canopy, letting light flood in. Seedlings and young trees quickly grow to fill the gap.

In one hectare of forest 1500 species of plant can be found. Lianas climb up to the canopy to produce their own crowns. Birds, mammals, and insects pollinate the trees. The trees' branches and trunks are covered in ferns and mosses. Medicines, coffee, rubber, and chocolate, come from rainforest plants.

EMERGENT TREES ARE 100 METRES TALL – ALMOST TWICE AS HIGH AS THE CANOPY BELOW

MANY BIRDS, SUCH AS THIS TOUCAN, EAT FRUITS THAT GROW IN THE TREES

SPIDER MONKEYS FEED IN THE TREE-TOPS, SPREADING SEEDS FAR AROUND

LIANAS CLIMB TO REACH THE LIGHT

MOST OF THE LEAVES ARE SPECIALLY SHAPED SO THAT THEY CATCH RAINWATER AND POUR IT OFF AT THEIR TIPS

RAFFLESIA IS A PARASITE THAT LIVES ON LIANA ROOTS AND HAS THE LARGEST OF ALL FLOWERS

BROMELIAD LEAVES CATCH AND HOLD WATER – DEAD INSECTS DECAY IN THE WATER PROVIDING NUTRIENTS FOR THE PLANT

STRANGLER FIGS ARE CARRIED UP TO THE LIGHT BY GROWING TREES, WHICH THE STRANGLER FIGS SURROUND AND EVENTUALLY KILL

THE CANOPY

THE UNDERSTOREY LIES BENEATH THE CANOPY

FUNGI HELP DEAD WOOD AND LEAVES TO ROT

FALLEN LEAVES QUICKLY ROT AWAY TO FORM A THIN SOIL

STRONG, WIDE BUTTRESS ROOTS SUPPORT THE HUGE TREE

Forest Growth

FORESTS ARE communities of trees and other plants. Many different kinds of forest grow, depending on the types of plants, the climate, terrain, and soil, and the influence of humans and other animals. Forests develop over tens, or even millions, of years – they are at the end of a long succession (sequence of changes) in which different plants take over. On bare soil, 'opportunist' plants soon appear. They are well-adapted to exploiting new ground. Over time, other species replace them. This plant succession usually leads to forests, like the beech forest shown here. Forests are called climax communities because they are at the end of a succession.

Plant defences

Plants are a source of food for many animals. To defend themselves from herbivores (plant-eaters), many plants use poisons, a tough skin, spines, or thorns. Nettles use fine, needle-sharp hairs. These pierce the animals' skin and break, releasing a tiny amount of painful, stinging acid. Large animals that would otherwise eat nettles soon learn to leave them alone.

NEEDLE-SHARP NETTLE HAIRS

1) Bare ground
Bare or cleared chalky ground is soon invaded by quick-growing annual plants. Other species then arrive.

OTHER PLANTS INVADE, AND REPLACE THE 'OPPORTUNISTS'

THE NEW CARPET OF PLANTS INCLUDES THYME, CLOVER, MILKWORT, AND GRASSES

RABBITS GRAZE, KEEPING THE CHALK GRASSLAND PLANTS SMALL

A DENSE SCRUB OF DOGWOOD, ROSE, AND HAWTHORN BUSHES DEVELOPS

① ② ③

BARE CHALKY SOIL – READY FOR PIONEER PLANTS TO COLONIZE THE LAND

RAGWORT, COLTSFOOT, AND MOSSES ARE OPPORTUNISTS INVADING THE BARE GROUND

2) Chalk grassland
Grazing by rabbits and sheep, and also cutting by humans, helps to develop a rich carpet of growth. Many of the plants are specially adapted to living on the chalky soil.

3) Scrub
Where there is little or no grazing, woody plant species invade. Bushes form a dense scrub which creates too much shade for delicate grassland plants to grow.

THE CROWNS OF THE BEECH TREES REACH UPWARDS FOR SUNLIGHT

A BEECH FOREST FINALLY DEVELOPS AT THE END OF A LONG SUCCESSION

4) Ash wood

Ash trees form their own wood-land. Sheltered beneath the canopy of ash trees, beech seeds can germinate and grow. The ash trees act as a nursery for these slower growing trees.

ASH TREES HAVE SPACED OUT LEAVES SO SUNLIGHT CAN REACH THE GROUND AND NEW PLANTS CAN GROW

5) Beech forest

The leaves of the beech trees shade the soil below. Little else grows here except for special plants like dog's mercury. Where there is enough light, brambles and nettles flourish.

DOG'S MERCURY

DEAD PLANT AND ANIMAL MATERIAL SLOWLY CHANGES INTO NUTRIENT-RICH SOIL – TREES USE THE NUTRIENTS FOR GROWTH

YOUNG BEECH BEGIN TO GROW WITH THE HELP OF THE ASH TREES

FEW PLANTS GROW IN THE SHADE OF THE BEECH TREES

BRAMBLES AND NETTLES HAVE STINGS AND SPIKES TO STOP THEM BEING EATEN

Mountain Zones

THE HIGHER you climb up a mountain, the colder the climate gets. Prevailing winds affect the climate too, making it wetter on one side of the mountain than the other. The wind and rain, and changes in temperature with height, create different vegetation zones on a mountain. In central Africa the lowland plains at the foot of a mountain are dominated by savanna grassland and acacia woodlands. Between 1500 and 2400 metres, moist, high rainforest flourishes. Above this, mountain bamboo is the dominant vegetation. Higher still, sub-alpine moorland extends up to about 4000 metres. Beyond this lies the Afro-alpine zone, where the days are warm and the nights are cold. From 4800 metres to the bleak summit, there is little or no vegetation except for scattered lichens.

Mountain rainfall
Moisture-rich winds are forced up the mountain side. This causes the moisture to condense as clouds, which form mists. When there is too much moisture in the air, it falls as rain, sleet, or snow. This effects the pattern of the vegetation zones.

Bamboo belt
Between 2400 and 3000 metres, mountain bamboo forms a dense vegetation up to 15 metres in height. These giant grasses grow from rhizomes. They grow so densely that sunlight is unable to get through to the ground.

BAMBOO HAS FAST GROWING WOODY STEMS

Afro-alpine zone
Above 4000 metres plants have to protect themselves against the frost that forms at night and melts during the day. White hairs keep ice off the plant's skin and absorb the sun's warmth. Some plants grow close to the ground for shelter. The hyrax, a small, hoofed mammal, lives amongst the rocks.

TREE-DAISY LEAVES HAVE SILVERY HAIRS TO REDUCE HEAT LOSS

IN THE AFRO-ALPINE ZONE MANY PLANTS HUG THE GROUND FOR WARMTH

ABOVE THE BAMBOO ZONE, LARGE SHRUB-LIKE HEATHERS GROW IN THE MOORLAND ZONE

Savanna
The hot, dry lowlands are covered in savanna grasslands. Only drought-resistant grasses and trees grow here. In the rainy season there is lots of growth, providing food for many animals.

In the dry season, hot winds dry the vegetation so much that fires are common (caused by lightning and people). But after a fire, acacia trees soon sprout, and grasses emerge again from underground.

THE TREE CANOPY OF THE HIGH RAINFOREST

ACACIA WOODLAND MERGES WITH RAINFOREST AS RAINFALL INCREASES WITH HEIGHT

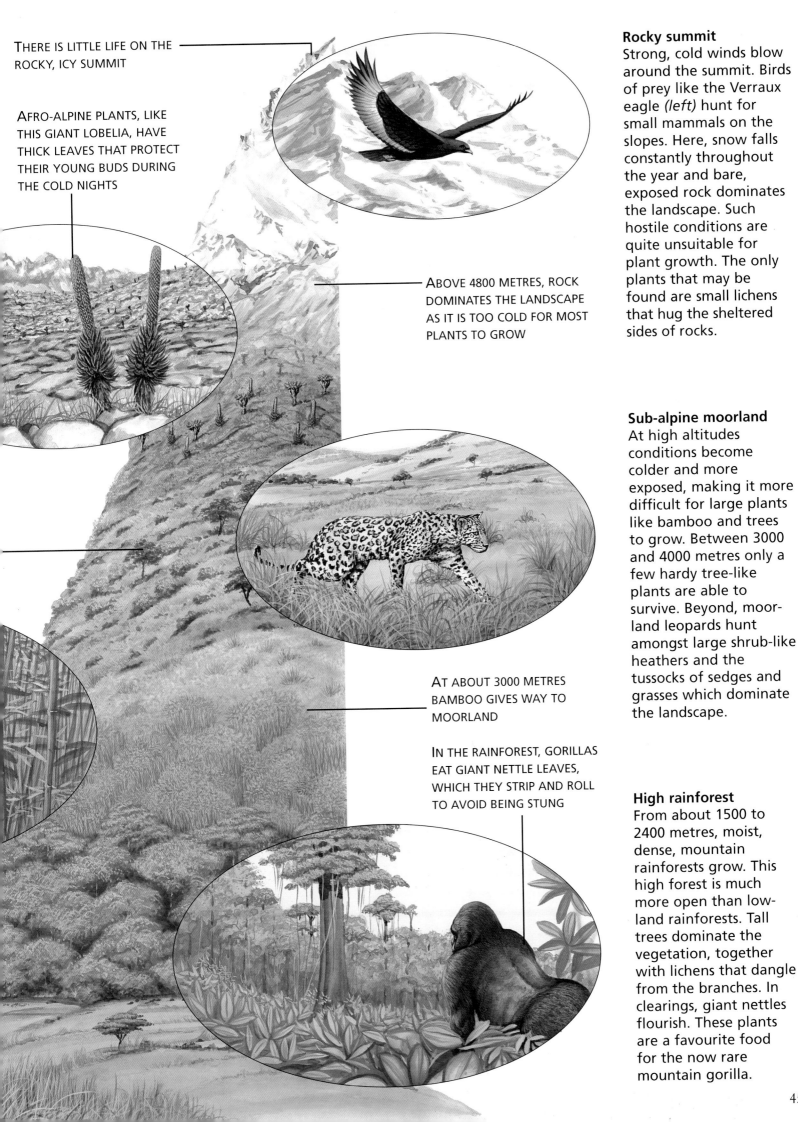

THERE IS LITTLE LIFE ON THE ROCKY, ICY SUMMIT

AFRO-ALPINE PLANTS, LIKE THIS GIANT LOBELIA, HAVE THICK LEAVES THAT PROTECT THEIR YOUNG BUDS DURING THE COLD NIGHTS

ABOVE 4800 METRES, ROCK DOMINATES THE LANDSCAPE AS IT IS TOO COLD FOR MOST PLANTS TO GROW

AT ABOUT 3000 METRES BAMBOO GIVES WAY TO MOORLAND

IN THE RAINFOREST, GORILLAS EAT GIANT NETTLE LEAVES, WHICH THEY STRIP AND ROLL TO AVOID BEING STUNG

Rocky summit

Strong, cold winds blow around the summit. Birds of prey like the Verraux eagle (left) hunt for small mammals on the slopes. Here, snow falls constantly throughout the year and bare, exposed rock dominates the landscape. Such hostile conditions are quite unsuitable for plant growth. The only plants that may be found are small lichens that hug the sheltered sides of rocks.

Sub-alpine moorland

At high altitudes conditions become colder and more exposed, making it more difficult for large plants like bamboo and trees to grow. Between 3000 and 4000 metres only a few hardy tree-like plants are able to survive. Beyond, moorland leopards hunt amongst large shrub-like heathers and the tussocks of sedges and grasses which dominate the landscape.

High rainforest

From about 1500 to 2400 metres, moist, dense, mountain rainforests grow. This high forest is much more open than lowland rainforests. Tall trees dominate the vegetation, together with lichens that dangle from the branches. In clearings, giant nettles flourish. These plants are a favourite food for the now rare mountain gorilla.

Index